THE WACKIEST JOKE BOOK EVER!

THE WACKIEST JOKE BOOK EVER

Copyright © 2017 Portable Press

All rights reserved. No part of this publication may be reproduced, distributed, or transmitted in any form or by any means, including photocopying, recording, or other electronic or mechanical methods, without the prior written permission of the publisher, except in the case of brief quotations embodied in critical reviews and certain other noncommercial uses permitted by copyright law.

Portable Press
An imprint of Printers Row Publishing Group
10350 Barnes Canyon Road, Suite 100, San Diego, CA 92121
www.portablepress.com
e-mail: mail@portablepress.com

Printers Row Publishing Group is a division of
Readerlink Distribution Services, LLC.
Portable Press is a registered trademark of
Readerlink Distribution Services, LLC.

All correspondence concerning the content of this book should
be addressed to Portable Press,
Editorial Department, at the above address.

Publisher: Peter Norton
Publishing/Editorial Team: Vicki Jaeger,
Tanya Fijalkowski, Lauren Taniguchi
Editorial Team: JoAnn Padgett, Melinda Allman,
J. Carroll, Dan Mansfield
Production Team: Jonathan Lopes, Rusty von Dyl

Collected and curated by Kim T. Griswell
Cover and interior concept by Patrick Merrell
Cover by Rusty von Dyl
Interior by SunDried Penguin

ISBN 978-1-62686-380-4

Printed in the United States of America

First Printing: May 2017
21 20 19 18 17   1 2 3 4 5

1

FAMILY FUNNIES

Why was the mother firefly unhappy?

Her children weren't very bright.

What does the Pickle family do when their car breaks down?

They dill with it.

FAMILY FUNNIES

Why did the kid leave cheese beside the computer?

To feed the mouse.

Mom: Did you take a shower this morning?

Kid: Why? Is one missing?

Sis: When did you lose your two front teeth?

Bro: I didn't. They're in my pocket.

Who is bigger, Mrs. Bigger or her baby?

Her baby is a little Bigger.

FAMILY FUNNIES

Dad: Why did you fail your history test?

Kid: All the questions were about things that happened before I was born.

Mama Giraffe: Eat your leaves, son. They put color in your cheeks.

Giraffe Son: Who wants green cheeks?

Why wasn't Mom worried about the moose in the kitchen?

It was a chocolate mousse.

Elephant Baby: Pops? Do elephants really have good memories?

Elephant Dad: I forget.

FAMILY FUNNIES

If you eat one half of an apple pie and your sister eats the other half, what are you left with?

A very angry mom.

Why did Ed's parents name their second son Ed, too?

Because two Eds are better than one.

Bro: I just spotted a leopard!

Sis: Don't be silly. Leopards are born that way.

Why don't dads ever buy new underwear?

Because *under*wear never gets worn *out*.

FAMILY FUNNIES

Grandma: I once typed an essay on the belly of a frog.

Grandkid: Wow! How'd you get the frog into the typewriter?

What's the best cure for sleepwalking?

Put tacks on the floor.

Dad: Why did you dip your computer in melted caramel?

Kid: I wanted a candied Apple.

How can you tell a baby snake?

By its rattle.

FAMILY FUNNIES

Why did Grandpa's hair turn gray before his moustache?

It was older.

Mom: I found a restaurant where we can eat dirt cheap!

Dad: I'd rather eat steak.

Who isn't your sister or brother but is still a child of your parents?

You.

What did the mama cow say to her calf?

Go to sleep! It's pasture bedtime.

FAMILY FUNNIES

Hey! There's a family of horses moving in next door!

Great! They'll make good nei-ei-ei-ghbors.

How many paws does a lion have?

One Paw. Just like everyone else.

What happened when the baby drank 8 colas?

He burped 7-Up.

Dad: Why are you eating your homework?

Kid: The teacher said it was a piece of cake.

FAMILY FUNNIES

What happened when Mom put too much mousse in her hair?

She grew antlers.

Why was the kid late to school every day?

The teacher said it was never too late to learn.

What's worse than a crying baby?

Two crying babies.

What did the mirror say to the dresser?

I see your drawers!

FAMILY FUNNIES

Why did Farmer John borrow a needle from his wife?

He couldn't find the one in the haystack.

Why did the kid put the cake in the freezer?

It needed icing.

Kid: How many apples grow on a tree?

Mom: All of them.

Do you have to be royal to ride in a carriage?

Not if you're a baby.

FAMILY FUNNIES

Which family member is purple?

Your grape grandmother.

Kid: Dad, which board do you need to finish the fence?

Dad: The last one.

Which relatives always come to family picnics?

The ants.

Which grade should you never get on a report card?

D. It makes Ma mad.

FAMILY FUNNIES

What is big and yellow and comes in the morning to brighten Mom's day?

The school bus.

Why did Dad work late at the pajama factory?

He was on the nightie shift.

Kid: What's the best way to avoid wrinkles?

Grandma: Don't sleep in your clothes.

Kid: Will the pancakes be long? I'm starving.

Dad: No. They'll be round.

FAMILY FUNNIES

What do you call rotten eggs, spoiled milk, and moldy bread?

Gross-eries.

Mom: How do you know the dog ate your homework?

Kid: I fed it to him.

What do you give a sick female relative?

Auntie-biotics.

Grandpa: I've been swimming since I was five years old.

Grandkid: You must be really tired.

2

ANIMAL SILLIES

What do whales chew?

Blubber gum.

What is black and white and green and black and white?

Two zebras fighting over a pickle.

ANIMAL SILLIES

What kind of animal lives in a can?

A cantaloupe.

Why did the elephant quit the circus?

He was tired of working for peanuts.

Who wrote *The Worst Joke Book Ever*?

Terry Bull.

What is white on the outside, yellow in the middle, and white on the outside?

A lion sandwich.

ANIMAL SILLIES

What is black and white and red all over?

A zebra hiding in a bottle of ketchup.

How are playing cards like wolves?

They both travel in packs.

What one-horned animal won't take "no" for an answer?

The why-nocerous.

Why do giraffes have such long necks?

Because their feet stink.

ANIMAL SILLIES

Why did the watchdog sleep all the time?

His owner forgot to wind him.

Why are there no aardvarks in Alaska?

They can't afford the plane fare.

What was the silly chicken doing in the garden?

Sitting on an eggplant.

What do you call a dog that sneezes?

A germy shepherd.

ANIMAL SILLIES

What do you call a bunny that gives out parking tickets?

Meter Rabbit.

Why wouldn't the horse talk to the cow?

Everything she said was udder nonsense.

Where do cows go on vacation?

Moo York.

Why did the hippo sit on a pumpkin?

He wanted to play squash.

ANIMAL SILLIES

What do baby bunnies learn in school?

The alfalfa-bet.

What's the difference between a platypus and a peanut butter sandwich?

A platypus doesn't stick to the roof of your mouth.

Why do squirrels live in trees?

To avoid all the nuts on the ground.

How do dogs keep up on local news?

Smellovision.

ANIMAL SILLIES

How does a polite lion greet a hunter?

"Pleased to eat you!"

What is the biggest ant?

The elephant!

Which animal never remembers names?

The owl. It's always saying, "Who? Who?"

What's the best use of cowhide?

To keep the cow together.

ANIMAL SILLIES

How do you know there's an elephant in your sandwich?

It's too heavy to lift.

How do fish buy things online?

With a credit cod.

Which bird is always out of breath?

A puffin.

Why did the dog go to jail?

He didn't pay his barking ticket.

ANIMAL SILLIES

Why do rabbits have fur coats?

Because they'd look silly in leather jackets.

Why don't polar bears live in the desert?

They can't bear the heat.

How many kinds of gnus are there?

Two. Good gnus and bad gnus.

What do you call an elephant in a phone booth?

Stuck.

ANIMAL SILLIES

How can you keep milk from spoiling?

Leave it in the cow.

How can you tell which end of a worm is its head?

Tickle it in the middle and see which end laughs.

What do you get if you cross a barber with a sheep?

A baa-aa-aad haircut.

How do you get fur from a bear?

Run as fast as you can!

ANIMAL SILLIES

Why did the ram fall off the cliff?

It didn't see the ewe turn.

What is a skunk's favorite sandwich?

Peanut butter and smelly.

Why did the cow stop giving milk?

She wasn't in the moooooo-d.

What do you call a canine magician?

A labracadabrador.

ANIMAL SILLIES

Why do ducks make the best detectives?

They always quack the case.

What did the near-sighted porcupine say to the cactus?

"Hi, Mom!"

What do alligators call children?

Appetizers.

What do dogs eat at the movies?

Pupcorn.

3

SILLYSAURUS

What kind of dinosaur wears a cowboy hat and boots?

Tyrannosaurus tex.

Why did the raptor paint its claws yellow?

So it could hide in the banana tree.

SILLYSAURUS

What goes "thump, squish, thump, squish"?

A T. rex with one wet sneaker.

Which dinosaur has the biggest vocabulary?

A Thesaurus.

What is a dinosaur's favorite snack?

Macaroni and trees.

Which dinosaur demolishes buildings?

Tyrannosaurus wrecks.

SILLYSAURUS

What do you call a dinosaur that stubs its toe?

Sore-toe-a-saurus.

Did you hear the one about the pterodactyl egg?

It was a very old yolk.

Why did the plesiosaur eat a fleet of ships carrying potatoes?

Because no one can eat just one potato ship.

What do you get when you cross a dinosaur and a wizard?

Tyrannosaurus hex.

SILLYSAURUS

What was the world's fastest dinosaur?

The prontosaurus.

How do you tell a dinosaur to hurry?

"Shake a leg-osaurus!"

Why are dinosaurs big, green, and scaly?

If they were small, yellow, and fuzzy they would be tennis balls.

Why did the stegosaurus climb a tree?

Because the sign said
KEEP OFF THE GRASS.

SILLYSAURUS

What is T. rex's favorite game?

Swallow the leader.

Why did the pterodactyl cross the road?

Because there weren't any chickens yet.

Why shouldn't you teach T. rex to add 4 + 4?

You might get 8 (ate).

Which dinosaur keeps you awake at night?

The bronto-snore-us.

SILLYSAURUS

What follows a stegosaurus wherever it goes?

Its tail.

What do you get if you give a dinosaur a pogo stick?

Big holes in your driveway.

What do you call the king of the dinosaurs after it evolves into a chicken?

Tyrannosaurus pecks.

Why did the sauropod wear purple pajamas?

Because its pink ones were in the wash.

SILLYSAURUS

What kind of dinosaur has no wings, but flies all over?

The kind that needs a bath.

How do you get down from a dinosaur?

You don't! You get down from a goose.

What time is it when a dinosaur sits on your toilet?

Time to get a new toilet.

Which dinosaur was a crybaby?

Tear-annosaurus rex.

SILLYSAURUS

**What do you do
with a yellow triceratops?**

Teach it to be brave.

**What was the brontosaurus's
favorite game?**

Squash.

What does a triceratops sit on?

Its tricera-bottom.

Why did T. rex cross the road?

To eat the chickens on the other side.

SILLYSAURUS

What do you call a polite dinosaur?

A please-iosaur.

Why are dinosaurs always found in the ground?

Because they couldn't climb trees.

Which dinosaur caught the worm?

Archaeopteryx. It was an early bird.

What kind of dinosaurs live in graveyards?

Cemetery-dactyls.

SILLYSAURUS

Why do museums have so many old dinosaur bones?

They can't find any new ones.

Why did the dinosaur eat a cow and three ducks?

It liked milk and quackers.

What do you do when a dinosaur breaks its toe?

Call a very big toe truck.

What do you call a T. rex having a temper tantrum?

Brat-T rex.

SILLYSAURUS

Why invite a dinosaur to your birthday party?

They're tons of fun.

Why did dinosaurs become extinct?

They didn't want to hear any more dinosaur jokes.

Where was the dinosaur when the sun went down?

In the dark.

Why did the apatosaurus devour the factory?

She was a plant eater.

SILLYSAURUS

Which dinosaurs make the best police officers?

Tricera-cops.

When is a dinosaur likely to enter your house?

When the door is open.

What's bright blue and weighs 2,000 pounds?

A dinosaur holding its breath.

How long were a velociraptor's legs?

Long enough to reach the ground.

4

ODDBALLS

How do you make a hot dog stand?

Steal its chair.

What is the first thing a ball does when it stops rolling?

It looks round.

ODDBALLS

What do you call a six-foot-tall basketball player?

Shortie.

What is stranger than seeing a catfish?

Seeing a goldfish bowl.

What can you serve but never eat?

A tennis ball.

Why are baseball games played at night?

Because bats sleep during the day.

ODDBALLS

What's the bounciest room in a palace?

The ballroom.

Why did the umpire throw the chicken out of the game?

He suspected fowl play.

Why can't pigs play basketball?

They hog the ball.

What are the last words of "The Star Spangled Banner"?

Play ball!

ODDBALLS

Why are fish lousy at volleyball?

They run away from the net.

What is harder to catch the faster you run?

Your breath.

What does an umpire always do before he eats?

Brushes off the plate.

Soccer player: I could kick myself for missing that goal.

Teammate: Don't bother. You'll probably miss.

ODDBALLS

What did the batter say when the coach called in a new pitcher?

That's a relief!

How is a baseball catcher like a farmer?

They both chase fowls.

Why are basketballs always wet?

The players dribble a lot.

Why do golfers like to eat Cheerios?

Because there's a hole in every one.

ODDBALLS

How are football players like pilots?

They both make touchdowns.

What's the difference between a bad goalie and Cinderella?

Cinderella got to the ball.

Mom: Which player is the fullback?

Kid: The one who ate too much before the game.

Which three letters will stop a quarterback sneak?

I-C-U!

ODDBALLS

What bird can be found at the end of every race?

The puffin.

What did the dog say when a ball landed on top of the house?

Roof! Roof!

How do you keep squirrels off the football field?

Hide the ball. It drives them nuts!

Which sport is the quietest?

Bowling. You can hear a pin drop.

ODDBALLS

Wide receiver: What's the best way to catch a ball?

Coach: Have someone throw it to you.

Why did Cinderella lose the tennis tournament?

She had a pumpkin for a coach.

When do baseball players wear armor?

For knight games.

Golfer: Golf is a funny game.

Caddy: It's not supposed to be.

ODDBALLS

What is a basketball player's favorite kind of story?

Tall tales.

What's the funniest baseball team?

The New York Prankees.

What do you call a girl who stands in the middle of a volleyball court?

Annette.

Coach: You'd be better at bowling than baseball.

Kid: Why?

Coach: You always get strikes!

ODDBALLS

Why did the football fan go to the bathroom?

He wanted to watch the Toilet Bowl.

What's a basketball player's favorite snack?

Cookies, because they can dunk them.

Why did the baseball player keep winking?

He needed batting practice.

Why did the chicken cross the baseball field?

The umpire called a fowl.

ODDBALLS

Sports stories:

Extra Innings by Willy Win, illustrated by Betty Wont

What has 18 legs and catches flies?

A baseball team.

Where do old bowling balls end up?

In the gutter.

How do hens root for their favorite football team?

They egg them on.

ODDBALLS

Why did the shortstop get arrested?

He was caught stealing third base.

**Why do porcupines win
every ball game?**

They have the most points.

5

THAT'S HISTORICAL!

Who was America's funniest Founding Father?

Benjamin Pranklin.

Where was Queen Elizabeth II crowned?

On her head.

THAT'S HISTORICAL!

Teacher: For tonight's homework, write an essay on Abraham Lincoln.

Student: I'd rather write on paper.

Who was France's sleepiest emperor?

Nap-oleon.

Which American president wore the biggest shoes?

The one with the biggest feet.

Which Egyptian queen loved spaghetti?

Cleo-pasta.

THAT'S HISTORICAL!

How was Thomas Jefferson like a fish?

He was a flounder of his country.

Why did Paul Revere always carry a handkerchief?

He was the town crier.

Why was Queen Elizabeth I buried at Westminster Abbey?

Because she was dead.

Which patriotic song comes in handy when you sneeze?

Hanky Doodle Dandy.

THAT'S HISTORICAL!

What did Pocahontas become on her 21st birthday?

A year older.

Who invented the first airplane that didn't fly?

The Wrong brothers.

Who was purple and conquered the world?

Alexander the Grape.

Where is Timbuktu?

Between Timbuk-one and Timbuk-three.

THAT'S HISTORICAL!

Why did Teddy Roosevelt throw away his sleeping bag?

He couldn't get it to wake up.

Which president was the best social-networker?

Abraham LinkedIn.

How were the Pilgrims like ants?

They lived in colonies.

Which famous French landmark can't stand up?

The Eiffel (I fell) Tower.

THAT'S HISTORICAL!

What's the smelliest statue in Egypt?

The Stynx.

Which Leonardo da Vinci painting won't stop complaining?

The Moaning Lisa.

What did Benjamin Franklin say when he discovered electricity?

Nothing. He was too shocked.

Why didn't the lookout on the *Titanic* spot the iceberg?

He had bad ice sight.

THAT'S HISTORICAL!

Which telephone inventor had a cookie named after him?

Alexander Graham Cracker.

Which Roman emperor always had a cold?

Julius Sneezer.

Who was the world's smartest pig?

Ein-swine.

What part of London is in China?

The letter "n."

THAT'S HISTORICAL!

If Genghis Khan were alive today, what would he be most famous for?

His age.

How did George Washington cross the Delaware?

In a boat.

Where can you find Moscow?

In the barn next to Pa's cow.

What do Alexander the Great and Winnie the Pooh have in common?

Their middle name.

THAT'S HISTORICAL!

How often do ships like the *Titanic* sink?

Just once.

Two wrongs don't make a right, so what do two rights make?

An airplane.

What did Sir Lancelot wear to bed?

A knight gown.

Which soldiers traveled the most?

The Romans.

THAT'S HISTORICAL!

How is the United States like a healthy kid?

Both have good constitutions.

Why was Billy the Kid sitting on his mother's stove?

He wanted to be home on the range.

Where was the Treaty of 1783 signed?

At the bottom.

What happened when an apple hit Sir Isaac Newton on the head?

He realized the gravity of the situation.

THAT'S HISTORICAL!

Why don't you ever hear about Betsy Ross?

Interest in her has flagged.

Is the capital of Missouri pronounced Saint Loo-is or Saint Loo-ey?

Neither. It's pronounced Jefferson City.

How do we know the ancient Romans were smart?

They understood Latin.

What's the capital of Pennsylvania?

P.

THAT'S HISTORICAL!

How would a robber get gold out of Fort Knox?

Through the door.

What was the closest thing to King George III?

His underwear.

What happened to the inventor of sandpaper?

He had a rough time.

What stands in New York harbor and sneezes all day?

The Achoo of Liberty.

TOAD-ALLY WACKY

What is green and red all over?

A frog holding its breath.

Why couldn't the lizard stop singing?

He was a rap-tile.

TOAD-ALLY WACKY

What's green and bumpy and jumps a lot?

A cucumber with hiccups.

How do you catch a baby frog?

With a toad-pole.

How is a toad like a brick?

Neither one can play the trumpet.

What kind of lizard tells jokes?

A stand-up chameleon.

TOAD-ALLY WACKY

Why did the frog think it was a bird?

Because it was pigeon-toad.

What do you get when you cross a turtle with a sheep?

A turtle-neck sweater.

How many witches does it take to change a lightbulb?

One...but she changes it into a toad!

Diner: Waiter! Why is there a frog in my soup?

Waiter: Looks like it's eating the fly.

TOAD-ALLY WACKY

What do frogs always catch during baseball games?

Pop flies.

What do you get when you cross a toad with a pig?

A wart-hog.

What did the toad say to the kangaroo?

I feel kinda jumpy today.
How about you?

What happens when you throw a toad into the ocean?

It gets toadally wet.

TOAD-ALLY WACKY

What do turtles do on their birthday?

Shellabrate!

What do you say if you meet a toad?

Wart's new?

What kind of frog can be found at the North Pole?

One that's toadally lost.

Why did the toad sit on a marshmallow?

So it wouldn't fall into the hot chocolate.

TOAD-ALLY WACKY

What's the funniest place in the frog pond?

The silly pad.

What do you get when you cross a toad with Luke Skywalker?

Star Warts.

Why can't you believe anything toads tell you?

They're am-*fib*-ians.

How do you get a frog to fly?

Buy it an airplane ticket.

TOAD-ALLY WACKY

What kind of slippers did Frogerella wear to the ball?

Open-toad.

What goes "ribbit, ribbit, thunk"?

A frog laughing its head off.

Why did the frog jump over the moon?

Because the cow was on vacation.

What did the frog say when it couldn't stop coughing?

Sorry, I have a person in my throat.

TOAD-ALLY WACKY

What's green and warty and goes up and down all day?

A toad in an elevator.

What happens if you swallow a toad?

You croak!

Why did the frog take the bus?

Its car got toad.

Where do toads hang their coats?

In the croakroom.

TOAD-ALLY WACKY

What do you get if you cross a toad with a crocodile?

Leaping lizards.

What goes "dit-dit-dot-croak, dit-dit-dot-croak"?

Morse toad.

What's the best way to catch a tadpole?

Have someone throw it at you.

Why did the boy put a mouse in his sister's bed?

He couldn't catch a toad.

TOAD-ALLY WACKY

What do you get when you cross an alligator with a pickle?

A croco-dill.

What do toads drink in winter?

Hot croako.

7

THAT'S BANANAS!

Why did the elephant stomp on the banana?

He wanted a banana splat!

Why aren't bananas lonely?

They always travel in bunches.

THAT'S BANANAS!

What is King Kong's favorite musical?

Little Orphan Banannie.

How do monkeys get downstairs?

They slide down the banana-ster.

Why didn't the monkey undress for its bath?

Because it was wearing a bathrobe.

What was the monkey's favorite ice cream?

Chocolate chimp.

THAT'S BANANAS!

Which side of a monkey has the most fur?

The outside.

What is long and yellow and always points north?

A magnetic banana.

Which monkeys can fly?

Hot air baboons.

Why couldn't the monkey open the piano?

The keys were inside.

THAT'S BANANAS!

What is yellow and wears a mask?

The Lone Banana.

What did the monkey say to the sleeping banana?

Stop snoring before you wake up the whole bunch.

Moviegoer: I can't believe how much your monkey liked that movie.

Lady with monkey: I can't either! He hated the book.

Why don't chimpanzees have tails?

So they won't get caught in revolving doors.

THAT'S BANANAS!

What's yellow and writes?

A ballpoint banana.

What do you call a monkey whose bananas were stolen?

Furious George.

What is yellow and goes up and down?

A banana in an elevator.

What kind of monkeys live at the North Pole?

Cold ones.

THAT'S BANANAS!

Why do monkeys have fur?

So their underwear won't show.

What did the banana say to the monkey?

Don't be silly—bananas can't talk!

What do you call two monkeys who hang over a window?

Kurt-n-Rod

How do you keep a monkey from going through the eye of a needle?

Tie a knot in its tail.

THAT'S BANANAS!

Why did the monkey put banana peels on his feet?

He needed a new pair of slippers.

What do you call a monkey that swims with crocodiles?

Dinner.

What's yellow and hairy?

A banana wearing a toupee.

What should you do if you find ten little monkeys sleeping on your bed?

Get a hotel room.

THAT'S BANANAS!

Why did the monkey try to eat its bicycle?

It had a banana seat.

Where do you find monkeys?

Depends on where you left them.

What do you call a 2,000-pound gorilla?

Sir.

Why did the monkey close its eyes when it looked in the mirror?

To see how it looked when it was asleep.

THAT'S BANANAS!

What lives in a vineyard and swings through the vines?

Tarzan of the Grapes.

How long should a monkey's legs be?

Long enough to reach the ground.

Why did the banana go out with a prune?

Because it couldn't get a date.

Why did the banana cross the road?

It was running away from the monkey.

THAT'S BANANAS!

Traci: Why do elephants paint their faces yellow?

Stacy: I don't know, why?

Traci: So they can hide in banana trees.

Stacy: That's silly! I've never seen an elephant in a banana tree.

Traci: See! It works!

What do you call a banana with wings?

A fruit fly.

What's the opposite of a gorilla?

A stop-rilla.

8
SPACE CADETS

What do you get when you cross an alien with a hot drink?

Gravi-tea.

Astronaut: Captain, we're going faster than the speed of sound.

Captain: What did you say?

SPACE CADETS

Why should you never insult a Martian?

It might get its feelers hurt.

What's the center of gravity?

The letter "v."

What do you do with a green alien?

Wait until he ripens.

Why didn't Little Bo Peep fly to Mars?

She couldn't find her space-sheep.

SPACE CADETS

What did the mouse pilot say to the shuttle passengers?

"This is your captain squeaking!"

If Martians live on Mars and Venusians live on Venus, what lives on Pluto?

Fleas!

Where do astronauts get their degrees?

From a mooniversity.

Favorite do-it-yourself book:

Space Travel by Bill Jerome Rocket

SPACE CADETS

**How do you tie your shoes
in outer space?**

With an astro-knot.

Which planet has the most cows?

The mooooo-n.

**Why did the shuttle pilot refuse
to take flying lessons?**

It was a crash course.

**Why did the astronaut let go
of her sundae?**

She wanted an ice-cream float.

SPACE CADETS

Where do you find black holes?

In black socks.

Why can't astronauts keep jobs?

They always get fired after training.

What do you get when you cross a chicken with an alien?

An eggstra-terrestrial.

What is a Jedi's favorite snack?

Obi-Wan Cannoli.

SPACE CADETS

Why don't aliens celebrate birthdays?

They don't want to give away their presence.

What did the astronaut say when she walked into the space shuttle?

"Ouch!"

How many letters are in the alphabet?

Twenty-four...because E.T. went home.

Why haven't astronauts visited Mars?

They haven't been invited.

SPACE CADETS

What do the planets get after orbiting the sun all day?

Dizzy.

How do you wash a space shuttle?

Fly it through a meteor shower.

Favorite tabloid tale:

I Saw an Alien by Omar Goodness

Why did the alien abduct a dachshund?

It wanted a down-to-Earth pet.

SPACE CADETS

Besides shooting stars, which other stars have tails?

Dory, Tigger, and Bambi.

What do you call a wizard in space?

A flying sorcerer.

What do you call a robot that takes the longest route?

R2-Detour.

What is fast, loud, and crunchy?

A rocket chip.

9 DON'T BEE SILLY!

Why do bees hum?

Because they don't know how to whistle.

Can bees fly in rain?

Only if they wear their yellow jackets.

DON'T BEE SILLY!

Why don't bees play baseball?

They're always too bees-y.

Why do bees walk on the ceiling?

If they walked on the floor, someone might step on them.

Doctor, Doctor! I keep seeing bees circling my head!

Don't worry. It's just a bug that's going around.

What's black and yellow and goes "zzub, zzub"?

A bee flying backward.

DON'T BEE SILLY!

Why is the letter "A" like a flower?

Because a bee always comes after it.

How do you know bees are happy?

They hum while they work.

Why do bees have sticky hair?

Because they use honeycombs.

What did the bee order at the fast-food joint?

A hum-burger.

DON'T BEE SILLY!

Who's a bee's favorite composer?

Bee-thoven.

What did the bee in the sauna say?

'Swarm in here!

What was the bee's favorite musical?

Stinging in the Rain.

What is a bee's favorite sport?

Rug-bee.

DON'T BEE SILLY!

Book Buzz:

Looking at Bees by Amos Skeeto

What do you get when you cross a skunk with a bee?

You get stung by a stinker.

What do you call a wasp?

A wanna-bee.

Where do you take a wasp with a broken wing?

The waspital.

DON'T BEE SILLY!

How do bees get to school?

They take the buzz.

What do you call a bee having a bad hair day?

A frizz-bee.

What comes after an April bee?

A May-bee.

What's black and yellow and flies above the clouds?

A bee in an airplane.

DON'T BEE SILLY!

What's worse than being a fool?

Fooling with a bee!

What kind of wasp can you wear?

A yellow jacket.

Who writes books for little bees?

Bee-trix Potter.

What buzzes and is wanted by the FBI?

A killer bee.

DON'T BEE SILLY!

How does a bee cut firewood?

With a buzz saw.

What do you get when you cross a sheep with a bee?

A baaaa-humbug.

Girl: I'd like to buy a bee.

Pet store owner: We don't sell bees.

Girl: Then why do you have one in your front window?

Which insect can't play football?

The fumble-bee.

DON'T BEE SILLY!

What kind of suit does a bee wear to work?

A buzz-ness suit.

Why did the bee go to the doctor?

It had hives.

What did the rose say to the bee?

Buzz off!

Which insect gets the best grade in English?

The spelling bee.

DON'T BEE SILLY!

What does a bee sit on?

Its bee-hind.

What did the robber say to the bee?

Your honey or your life.

What kind of phones do bees use?

Cell phones.

Where do bees go on vacation?

Stingapore.

10

SCARED SILLY

What happened when the werewolf swallowed the clock?

He got ticks.

Why wouldn't the vampire climb into his coffin at sunrise?

He was an all-day sucker.

SCARED SILLY

What are a zombie's least favorite letters?

D K (decay).

Where does Medusa go when she visits Arizona?

The Petrified Forest.

Why won't Bigfoot cross the road?

Because that's what chickens do.

Do mummies like to visit King Tut's tomb?

Naw…they wouldn't be caught dead there.

SCARED SILLY

Who's the best dancer at the monster ball?

The Boogieman.

What did one zombie say to the other zombie?

"Get a life!"

What does the Loch Ness Monster eat for breakfast?

Bagels and lochs.

Why do vampire bats use red markers?

They like to draw blood.

SCARED SILLY

What kind of monster is never around when you need him?

A wherewolf.

Where do mummies go for pizza?

Pizza Tut.

Why didn't the zombie lose its teeth?

It used toothpaste.

Why did King Kong climb the Empire State Building so quickly?

He had a plane to catch.

SCARED SILLY

Which artist has the most haunted paintings?

Vincent van Ghost.

How many vampires does it take to change a lightbulb?

None. They prefer the dark.

What kind of key opens a casket?

A skeleton key.

Why did Batman go to the pet store?

To buy a Robin.

SCARED SILLY

How does Dracula like his coffee?

De-coffin-ated.

Which three letters terrify the Invisible Man?

I-C-U.

What does Frankenstein do first thing every morning?

He wakes up.

Why does Bigfoot always leave behind footprints?

Because they're dirty.

SCARED SILLY

Why do dragons love knights?

Because they're crunchy and good with ketchup.

What do you call two witches who share an apartment?

Broom-mates.

What did the mommy ghost say to the baby ghost?

Don't spook until you're spooken to.

How did the zombie feel after partying all night?

Dead on his feet.

SCARED SILLY

What is King Kong's favorite sandwich?

Go-rilla cheese.

How does a witch tell time?

With a witch watch.

Why doesn't the mummy take a vacation?

Because if he relaxes too much, he'll unwind.

Why did Dracula run around his coffin?

To catch up on his sleep.

SCARED SILLY

Where do ghosts like to swim?

The Dead Sea.

What was the pirate's favorite fish?

The swordfish.

Where do vampires keep their money?

In blood banks.

How could the Mummy have a brother if the Mummy's brother had no brothers?

The Mummy is a woman.

SCARED SILLY

Why did the Wolfman scratch himself?

No one else knew where he itched.

Why didn't the skeleton kid like to go to school?

Her heart wasn't in it.

When is it bad luck to have a black cat cross your path?

When you're a mouse.

How did the Phantom of the Opera get out of a locked room?

He played the piano until he found the right key.

SCARED SILLY

What is Dracula's favorite fast food?

Fangfurters.

What has two arms, two wings, three heads, and eight legs?

A man riding a horse holding a chicken.

Where did the Headless Horseman find his head?

In the last place he looked.

Who's the clumsiest monster?

Clodzilla.

SCARED SILLY

Why was the photographer arrested?

Because he shot people and then blew them up.

Why did Godzilla wrap a long string around a Japanese city?

He wanted a Tokyo-yo.

Why do zombies dine at the fanciest restaurants?

They only eat gore-met food.

Is Ghostland a country?

No. It's a terror-tory.

SCARED SILLY

Why did Bigfoot Jr. shave off all his hair?

He wanted to be a little bare (bear).

What's the first thing ghosts do when they get into a car?

They boo-ckle up.

What is a sea monster's favorite lunch?

A submarine sandwich.

Why do witches fly on broomsticks?

They're too lazy to walk.

SCARED SILLY

What do you call a zombie track team?

The Running Dead.

What's a cannibal's favorite pizza?

Cheese, with everyone on it.

What is sweet, brown, and deadly?

Shark-infested chocolate pudding.

What was the baby zombie's favorite toy?

Its heady bear.

EXTRA WACKY

Why couldn't Cinderella go to King Neptune's ball?

She didn't have a ferry godmother.

What is round and has a bad temper?

A vicious circle.

EXTRA WACKY

What should you do if you break your arm in two places?

Stay away from those places.

What is Tigger's favorite hot dog?

Wienie the Pooh

Patient: My ear's ringing. What should I do?

Doctor: Answer it.

What is a pig's favorite fairy tale?

Slopping Beauty.

EXTRA WACKY

Which animals are best at multiplication?

Rabbits.

What happened when the king's men told Humpty Dumpty a joke?

He fell for it.

Teacher: What is 5Q + 5Q?
Student: 10Q.
Teacher: You're welcome!

EXTRA WACKY

Painful Reading:

The Patient with the Exploding Bottom
by Stan Wellback

What do you call a boomerang that doesn't come back to you?

A bummerang.

How many skunks does it take to make a big stink?

A phew.

Why is lava red and hot?

Because if it were white and cold, it would be snow.

EXTRA WACKY

Did you know it takes three sheep to make one sweater?

I didn't even know they could knit!

What speaks every language?

An echo.

What do you get if you cross a dog with a chicken?

A pooched egg.

What did the skunk say when the wind changed?

It all comes back to me now.

EXTRA WACKY

Why are barns so noisy?

The cows have horns.

**Rooster #1 laid 3 eggs.
Rooster #2 laid 4 eggs.
How many eggs do you have?**

None. Roosters don't lay eggs.

What do you call a small billy goat?

A peanut butter.

Where can you find an ocean with no water?

On a map.

EXTRA WACKY

When is a worm safe from the early bird?

When it sleeps late.

What is 11 + 2 + 4 - 17?

A lot of work for nothing!

What do you call a boy with a car on his head?

Jack.

Patient: Doctor, Doctor! My nose is running.

Doctor: No. I think it's not.

EXTRA WACKY

**Did you hear about
the clothesline robbery?**

The underwear was held up by
two clothespins.

**What do you call
a three-footed aardvark?**

A yard-vark.

**What did the bear cub say when
his friend came to visit?**

I'd like you to meet my den mother.

Why did Miss Muffet need a map?

Because she lost her whey.

EXTRA WACKY

What kind of paper makes the best kites?

Flypaper

Zach: Josh is whispering in class.
Teacher: Why does that bother you?
Zach: I can't hear what he's saying.

Why did Captain Hook cross the road?

To get to the secondhand shop.

What do you call a tuba's father?

Ooom-papa.

EXTRA WACKY

How many bugs can you put in an empty pint jar?

One. After that, it's not empty.

What's the best brain food?

Noodle soup.

Why did the math teacher skip the chapter on circles?

They were pointless.

What happened when 19 and 20 got into a fight?

Twenty-one.

EXTRA WACKY

What makes kindergarten teachers so good?

They know how to make the little things count.

What sits on the ocean bottom and shakes?

A nervous wreck.

What's green and goes camping?

A brussels scout.

Stinkiest Book:

Too Many Beans by Wynn D. Bottom

EXTRA WACKY

What's pink and fluffy?

Pink fluff.

What's blue and pink and fluffy?

Pink fluff holding its breath.

What did one potato chip say to the other?

Let's go for a dip!

How do little shellfish travel?

By taxi crab.

EXTRA WACKY

Why did the driver hold his nose?

His car had gas.

What kind of pliers do you use in math?

Multipliers.

How much dirt is in a hole with a three-foot circumference?

None. Holes are empty.

Which cowboy lives in the ocean?

Billy the Squid.